James Steven

A Sermon Preached at the Ordination of the Rev. William

Nicol

To the Co-Pastoral Care of the Scots Church in Swallow Street, November

23, 1796

James Steven

A Sermon Preached at the Ordination of the Rev. William Nicol
To the Co-Pastoral Care of the Scots Church in Swallow Street, November 23, 1796

ISBN/EAN: 9783337021177

Printed in Europe, USA, Canada, Australia, Japan

Cover: Foto ©Lupo / pixelio.de

More available books at **www.hansebooks.com**

THE GOSPEL MINISTRY, *when improved*, THE
GREATEST BLESSING;
when resisted and abused, THE GREATEST CURSE.

A

S E R M O N

PREACHED AT

THE ORDINATION

OF THE

REV. WILLIAM NICOL,

TO THE CO-PASTORAL CARE OF THE SCOTS CHURCH
IN SWALLOW - STREET,

November 23, 1796.

BY THE

REV. JAMES STEVEN,

MINISTER OF THE SCOTS-CHURCH, CROWN-COURT,
COVENT-GARDEN.

To which is added

THE CHARGE

BY HENRY HUNTER, D. D.

OF THE SCOTS-CHURCH, LONDON-WALL.

London.

PRINTED FOR THE AUTHORS,

BY T. GILLET, BARTHOLOMEW-CLOSE;

And fold by DILLY, Pou'try; CADEL and DAVIS, Strand;
CHAPMAN, Fleet-Street; KAY, opposite Somerset-House,
Strand; and BISHOP, Newport-Street.

1796.

THE REV. DR. TROTTER,

THE REV. MR. NICOL,

MINISTERS ;

AND

To the Elders, and other Members of the Church in Swallow-Street.

———◅●▶———

MY CHRISTIAN FRIENDS,

HAD I confulted merely my *own* fentiments and feelings, the Sermon yefterday delivered would never have been fubmitted to public infpection. But your urgent, una-nimous requeft, followed up by that of fome refpectable Clergy of the Church of England, and of many other Minifters and Gentlemen pre-fent on the occafio n ,hath overpow-

A 3   ered

ered my reluctance, and given a *pub-licity* to the Difcourfe, which I little expected, and which it little merits.

I prefume not to ftart as a candidate for theological *fame*; my ambition is bounded by the wifh of being ufeful, and refpected, in the circle of my *more immediate* Connections. The Sermon has little elfe to recommend it than the importance of the fubject, and it's tendency to aroufe both the Preachers and Profeffors of Chriftianity, from that lethargic indifference, and dead formality, which fo ftrongly mark the complexion of the *Age*. Though it may, perhaps, obtain a *wider* circulation, it is now printed, as it was firft preached, with a *particular* view to the religious interefts of the Church

Church in Swallow-Street; which I
hope, through the connection yefterday formed, will be greatly pro-
moted, and long perpetuated. The
Difcourfe iffues from the *Prefs*, nearly
in the ftate in which it was delivered
from the *Pulpit*. Committing it,
fuch as it is, to *your ferious regard*,
to the *candour of the Public*, to the
difpofal and bleffing of the Great
Head of the Church, I am,

With unfeigned affection,

Your Servant in the Lord,

JAMES STEVEN.

Thornhaugh-Street, Bedford-Square,
Nov. 24, 1796.

THE SERVICE OF THE DAY
was conducted in the following Order:

———

The Rev. Mr. SMITH began with Prayer.

The Rev. Mr. LOVE read the Scriptures, gave the Narrative, and propofed the Queftions, ufual on fuch occafions.

The Rev. Mr. STEVEN preached the Sermon.

The Rev. Dr. TROTTER (Paftor of the Church) prayed the Confecration-Prayer, accompanied with the impofition of the hands of the Prefbytery.

The Rev. Dr. HUNTER gave the Charge; and

The Rev. Mr. RUTLEDGE concluded the whole, with Prayer and Thankfgiving.

A SERMON

ON

2 COR. II. 15, 16.

" FOR WE ARE UNTO GOD A SWEET SAVOUR OF
" CHRIST, IN THEM THAT ARE SAVED, AND
" IN THEM THAT PERISH: TO THE ONE, WE
" ARE THE SAVOUR OF DEATH UNTO DEATH;
" AND TO THE OTHER, THE SAVOUR OF LIFE
" UNTO LIFE."

EVER fince the Church of God was eftablifhed upon earth, a diftinct order of men has fubfifted in it, entrufted with the care of fouls, and with the miniftry of the Gofpel, as the means of fulfilling it. The facred nature of the office itfelf, the awful refponfibility attached unto it, the qualifications requifite to the right difcharge of it, and the vaft momentous confequences which muft for ever refult from it;—thefe are confiderations all fuited, on this occa-

fion,

fion, to ftrike our minds with an impreffive
energy. Than this, what ftation is more
dignified, more arduous, or, on which more
awful events intimately depend? If the
dignity of any function is to be eftimated,
by the *magnitude* of the end at which it
aims, or of the confequences to which it
leads; none is equal to that of the " Am-
baffadors of Chrift, who are allowed of God
to be put in truft with the Gofpel," and
fent " in Chrift's ftead, to befeech' men to
be reconciled unto God." What is the
employment of a Pnyfician, of a Lawyer, of
any Magiftrate or Minifter of State, (refpectable as they are) compared to that of a
faithful Minifter of " the Prince of Peace,
of the Lord of Glory?" *Theirs* relates only
to the bodily health, to the worldly pro-
perty, to the civil and political rights of
mankind; *his* embraces the vaft interefts of
their immortal fpirits, and its confequences,
furviving time, fhall extend even to Eternity itfelf.

Nothing can equal the dignity, except
the *comfort* arifing from the fuccefsful difcharge

charge of minifterial duty. To this, no true fervant of Chrift can be at all indifferent. He who feels no intereft, nor folicitude, refpecting the fuccefs of his miniftry, has reafon to conclude, that he is neither qualified, nor called to undertake it. Not that I would be underftood, as reprefenting great ufefulnefs, to be the only teft of a *valid* miniftry; I mean merely to affert, that this is what every true Minifter will eagerly defire and labour to attain,—that when attained he will rejoice, and that when awanting, he will be filled with the bittereft grief.

The context brings into view an illuftrious inftance of this kind, in the temper and conduct of the great Apoftle of the Gentiles. Reviewing his toils and travels in fpreading the Gofpel, he particularly records, to the honour of God, the fignal fuccefs wherewith he was favoured, at Troas, Macedonia, and other places where " a door was opened unto him, of the Lord." The very retrofpect of fuch a fcene of ufefulnefs, gladdened his heart, and made his joy fwell
into

into all the tranfports of exultation and triumph. " Now thanks be unto God," fays
he, " who always caufeth us to triumph
in Chrift, and maketh manifeft the favour
of his knowledge, by us, in every place."

Notwithftanding, however, the miracu-
lous powers by which his commiffion was
attefted, and notwithftanding the learning,
piety, eloquence, and zeal with which he
was fo fignally endowed; even Paul himfelf could not command *univerfal* fuccefs.
It was in the Apoftolic age, as in our own;
—" Some believed the things which were
fpoken, and fome believed not."* Though
many believed and turned unto the Lord,
multitudes refifted the word, and, through
unbelief and impenitence, perifhed in their
fins. A confideration this, which could
hardly fail to opprefs the benevolent breaft
of our Apoftle, and to damp the ardor of
that joy and gratulation, to which he had
juft been giving vent.

* Acts xxviii. 24.

Yet

Yet afflicted as he was with it, there were two thoughts, which banished or relieved the anguish of his mind. The one —that a Minister's final account will turn, not upon his *succefs*, but upon his *fincerity*; not upon the *good* which he hath done, but upon the *fidelity and diligence* difplayed in the attempt. The other—that he may faithfully fulfil the *end* of his Miniftry, even when thofe who fat under it, inftead of being faved, *perifh* for ever. What was primarily fpoken of the great Head and Prophet of the Church, in his official character, may apply to the abortive labours of every faithful fervant.—" I have laboured in vain, I have fpent my ftrength for nought, and in vain: yet furely my judgment is with the Lord, and my work with my God. Though Ifrael be *not* gathered, yet fhall I be g'orious in the eyes of the Lord, and my God fhall be my ftrength."* Long ago it was foretold of the foundation-ftone, which God himfelf hath laid in Zion —" this ftone is fet for the *fall*, as well as

* Ifaiah xlix. 5, 6.

for

for the rifing again of many in Ifrael."
This was the prediction of Him " who
knew the *end* from the beginning ;" and
did not *fact* exactly correfpond to it, Chriftianity would .be robbed of one of the main
.pillars, by which its truth and credibility are
fupported. As the fame fire that foftens
wax, hardens clay, as the fame light re-
frefhes the found, that hurts the weak dif-
tempered eye; fo the preaching of the Gofpel muft operate differently, on different
perfons, according to the reception given
unto it : It muft either prove " a favour
of death unto death, or a favour of life unto
life," unto all who hear it.

Employed, as we are this day, in the folemn defignation of our young Brother, to
the full exercife of his Chriftian Miniftry,
no fubject occurred to my mind, as more
adapted to the occafion, than that contained
in the words before us. They fuggeft the
two following points of difcuffion, to each
of which I would humbly claim your can-
did attention.

I. That

I. That Minifters, who faithfully diffufe " the fweet favour of the Knowledge of Chrift," are accepted of
God, *whatever* be the effect produced by their Miniftry.

II. That fince the preaching of the
Gofpel muft 'produce its effect, of
one kind or other, its hearers fhall
either *perifh* or *profit*, by their attendance upon it.

After a brief difcuffion of thefe two important points, I fhall *review and apply* the
whole, in a more direct reference to the bu-
finefs of the day.

The *Firft* truth taught us in the text, is
—that Minifters who faithfully diffufe the
" fweet favour of Chrift," are accepted of
God, *whatever* be the effect produced by
their Miniftry.

By an approved apoftolical pattern, we
are here inftructed in the great duty of a
Chriftian Minifter, which is—to make the
doctrine

doctrine of Chrift, the grand pervading theme of all his miniftrations, and to reprefent all the other lines of religious truth, as running and referring to this as the *centre*.

Though this fentiment needs not the aid of metaphor to render it intelligible, our Apoftle employs a ftriking, agreeable, and apt fimilitude, to give it luftre and advantage. He compares the preaching of the Gofpel, to a *rich perfume*, diffufing its fweet reviving fragrance all around.

Without ftraining, or doing violence to this beautiful image, I fhall ufe it no farther, than as it may illuftrate the fentiment, and ferve the purpofe in view.

Such as are converfant with Scripture phrafeology need not to be told, that, amongft many figurative allufions, that of a *precious, odoriferous ointment* is alfo ufed, to denote the Saviour's tranfcendent dignity, and the exquifite delight which his people feel, when hearing of his name. " Thy name,"

name," (fays the Church, fpeaking of
Chrift in his perfon, charaƈter, offices, and
grace) " thy name is as ointment pour-
ed forth." As though fhe had faid, " Not
more grateful to the external fenfes, not
more adapted is the moft delicious *perfume*
to re-animate a perfon fainting in a fwoon,
than are thy gracious excellencies to reftore
and delight my foul, when pining away under a fenfe of guilt, and under the preffure
of it's many fins, forrows, trials, and infirmities." From thefe, and other caufes,
every Chriftian, while he continues in the
body, is more or lefs fubjeƈt to many fpiritual maladies ; to much languor, debility,
and depreffion. In fuch circumftances,
what is the grand *Catholicon*, and where is
it to be found ? In vain do we feek for it
in the bleak, barren fields of human fcience;
in the claffical lore and cold fpeculations of
Orators, Philofophers, Poets, and Politi-
cians, either of ancient or modern date.—
No, " miferable comforters are they all!"
Nothing *they* can fuggeft can eafe an awakened confcience of it's cumbrous load, pa-
cify a troubled fpirit, revive and raife the
B foul

foul when drooping and disconsolate, or
satisfy it when panting for a happiness suit-
ed to it's nature.

The *Gospel*, and the Gospel *alone*, that
precious system of grace and consolation,
directs us to a suitable and effectual *Resto-
rative*; one sweeter far than all the odours
of Egypt and Arabia.—I need not say, I
mean the doctrine of *Christ*, and of *salvation through his blood.* To hearers of a
sound spiritual taste, "who have their senses
exercised, that they can discern between
good and evil," every other system must
be insipid, unsavoury, and useless; adapted
rather to *corrupt* than to *cure* a disordered,
imperfect, sinful nature.   And yet, strange
to tell! are there not some Preachers, if
such they may be called, whose discourses
smell more of *Socrates* and *Seneca*, of *Xe-
nophon* and *Plato*, than of that worthy name
by which alone sinners can be saved. Instead
of being " a sweet savour of Christ," neither the sentiment nor style of such Preachers has any *relish* of salvation in it.   By
fine-spun theories and maxims of morality,
by

by philofophical difquifitions on the beauty of virtue, and by the arts of fcience, *falfely fo called*, they think to reafon, or to charm the World into outward reformation. In-•ftead of pointing, like John, to " the Lamb of God, which taketh away the fin of the world," his name is but feldom and fparingly introduced, or if mentioned at all, it is with obvious reluctance and with cold referve.

Far otherwife acted Paul, and the other Apoftles, in fulfilling the Miniftry, which they had received of the Lord. They were " not afhamed of the Gofpel of *Chrift*," even of that part of it, which to others was the moft fhameful and offenfive. In the divine, though defpifed, doctrine of the Crofs, they were determined for ever to glory, becaufe well they knew, that though it might be fneered at, as foolifhnefs, by the felf-righteous of the age, " it was by this fame foolifhnefs of preaching that God was to fave them that believe." Wherever they went, this was their darling, delightful theme ; and almoft every where it was

crowned with remarkable. fuccefs. Tra-
verfing the land of Judea and of Paleſtine,
as well as the more remote, idolatrous nations, how freely did they impart to them
the Gofpel of God ? preaching to all " who
were called, both Jews and Greeks, Chriſt
the wifdom of God, and the power of God."
This they did, " not with the wifdom of
words, but with great plainnefs of fpeech,
left the Crofs of Chriſt ſhould become of
none effect." Inſtead of profelyting the Nations to the belief of the Truth by the glit-
ter of language, by the fallies of wit, or by
the charms of eloquence, they left it to it's
own innate evidence, to it's own in-
trinſic energy, that fo " the excellency of
the Power might appear to be *of God*."—
Nor did they mutilate and obfcure it, by
mingling fancies of their own, to make it
palatable to their hearers. This they left
to the Judaizing zealots, while they, with
undeviating integrity, " ſhunned not to declare *all* the counfel of God," without dar-
ing to conceal or to curtail the moſt trivial
part of it. On this Paul fpeaks, with an
air of triumph, in the verfe following the
text.

text.—" For we are not as many, who
corrupt the word of God : but as of fincerity, but as, of God, in the fight of God
fpeak we in Chrift."

The fame firmnefs and fidelity are expected, and will be ftudied of all, who
would imitate this approved, apoftolical
pattern. Would *we*, my reverend Fathers
and Brethren, wifh to fhare in the triumphs of this Apoftle, we muft feek it, by
eftablifhing the fame principles, by being
actuated with the fame motives, by aiming
at the fame end. To fhape and accommo-
date our Sermons to the humours of our
People, betrays a low, temporifing, daf-
tardly fpirit, unworthy of the truths we
preach, of the character we fuftain, and of
the exalted Mafter whom we ferve. Were
their filly prejudices and prepoffeffions to
guide us in the Pulpit, we behoved to walk
in a very partial and contracted range : too
much ftrefs would be laid upon fome doc-
trines and duties of Religion, while others
would be but flightly touched, or totally
concealed.

Inftead

Inftead of this meagre, defective plan, we are to lead our People through the land of Revelation, " in the length and in the breadth of it," explaining the hiftorical, prophetical, typical, doctrinal, and practical parts of it, in clofe connection with that " Great Myftery of Godlinefs," which reflects luftre, meaning, and confiftence on the whole. Treat we, for inftance, of the *Attributes* of God, we muft not fail to fhow, that it is *in the face of Chrift* that thefe fhine with their moft reviving fplendor. Treat we of the *Promifes*, we muft not forget to mention, that thefe are " all yea and amen *in Chrift*, to the glory of God." Speak we of the *Law* of God, in its moral obligation, demands, threatnings, and terrors, it would be highly culpable, did we omit to add, " Chrift is the end of the Law, for righteoufnefs, to every one that believeth." Do we infift on the *divine Commandments*, we muft inculcate and recommend obedience to thefe, only from arguments connected with Chrift, " without whom we can do nothing."—Thus, while we maintain " that faithful faying, and affirm

conftantly,

conftantly, that they who have believed in
God fhould be careful to maintain *good
works*," it will be in perfect harmony with
another " faithful faying, alfo worthy of
all acceptation—that *Chrift Jefus* came into
the world to *fave finners*, even the chief."

In this way will all our Miniftrations
literally prove " a fweet favour of *Chrift*;"
—his name will drop from our lips like the
fweet fmelling myrrh, fhedding forth the
moft rich, reviving fragrance. When the
Gofpel is thus preached, in it's native pu-
rity, and when it's great Author is thus
faithfully exhibited, in his infinite, unbor-
rowed, tranfcendant dignity, it might be
expected that men, in general, would be fo
convinced by it's evidence, and fo capti-
vated by it's charms, that, like Paul, they
would " count all things lofs, for the
excellency of the knowledge of Chrift Jefus." But fo it is, that from prejudice,
from pride of underftanding, from the
want of a found fpiritual tafte, to relifh and
receive it, *the doctrine of Chrift* is an *offence*
to many, who " reject the counfel of God

againft

againſt themſelves, and make light of the
great Salvation !"—Precious as Chriſt is
unto them that believe, unto the unbe-
lieving and impenitent, he hath always
been as " a root out of a dry ground ;" as
" having no form nor comelineſs in him,
wherefore he ſhould be deſired." Little do
perſons of this deſcription reflect on the
truth and meaning of that awful doom,
which our Lord, originally, denounced
againſt the *Jews* ; but which ſhall alſo
fall in juſt ſeverity upon all who are of the
ſame infidel-brood. " If ye believe not
that I am *He*, ye ſhall *die* in your ſins."
What elſe can be the portion of thoſe, that
will not come unto him, " who alone hath
the words of eternal life ? Dreadful doom !
who, that has any love to the ſouls of men,
would not deprecate and deplore it ; and
deploring, endeavour, to the utmoſt, to
prevent it ? Though his grief may be un-
availing, and his beſt-intended, beſt-direct-
ed efforts utterly abortive; he will be ready
to exclaim, in ſimilar ſtrains, with the
plaintive Prophet—" But if ye will not
hear, my ſoul ſhall weep in ſecret places
for

for your pride ; mine eye fhall weep fore,
and run down with tears *."

Under every difcouragement of this nature, the grand relief, to a faithful Minifter,
is—that, however offenfive may be his
Miniftry *unto Men*, it is accepted *of God*, as
a fervice *well-pleafing* in his fight. " We
are *unto God* (fays the Apoftle) a fweet favour of Chrift, both in them that are faved, and in them that perifh." Defirable
in itfelf, as it furely is, *fuccefs* in his work
is what no Minifter can command, or fe-
cure to himfelf ; it depends upon caufes,
over which he has no controul. Never-
thelefs, if he has endeavoured, by proper
means, to do good to the utmoft of his
power ; whether he fails or fucceeds in his
defign, " verily, he fhall in no wife lofe
his reward !" Indeed, in the tranquility
and approbation of confcience, and in the
refined, exalted pleafures connected with
it, the Redeemer's fervice may be faid to
be, its *own* reward. But, befides this recompence given *in hand*, every faithful

* Jer. xiii. 17.

Minifter

Minifter fhall gracioufly receive an ample
retribution, "at the refurrection of the
Juft." With whatever filence and obfcurity he may have paffed through life, he
fhall then be acknowledged and commend-
ed, before an affembled world ; and, from
his Mafter's lips, fhall openly receive that
grand *eulogium*, " Well done, good and
faithful fervant, enter thou into the joy of
thy Lord !"

It were well if his labours led to the
fame glorious iffue, in the cafe of *all,* who
attended on his Miniftry. But the iffues
and afpects of the Judgment-day will *vary*,
according as men have *rejected*, or *improved*
the means of falvation. This naturally leads
to the next topic of difcourfe.

II. That fince the preaching of the Gofpel muft produce it's effect, of one kind or
other, it's hearers fhall either *perifh* or
profit by their attendance upon it.

Firft, The text declares, that " to them
that perifh, it is *the favour of death unto
death*."

death." How awful and alarming the thought! that any who have heard the word of *life,* fhould *perifh* for ever—that, to any who have fat under the preaching of the Gofpel, it fhould ferve only as a *torch,* to light them down to the dreary abodes of *darknefs and defpair.* Not that this arifes from any fault or deficiency in the Gofpel itfelf, or that this is its direct and proper tendency. Entirely the reverfe—the effect is to be attributed, not to the Gofpel ; but to the unbelief, infenfibility, and obftinacy of finners themfelves, who " *will not* come unto Chrift, that they may have life, nor receive, with meeknefs, that ingrafted word, which is *able* to fave their fouls." In this view, we cannot impeach the wifdom and equity of the divine character, or fubject it to any imputation of harfhnefs and feverity. It is wholly matter of *felf*-crimination. Defpifers of " the Gofpel of the grace of God," may be faid to perifh *by choice* ; and, to *prefer* the miferies of fpiritual *death* to all the bleffednefs of endlefs *life!*

Permit

Permit me briefly to illuſtrate the truth of this ſentiment in two particulars.

1. When a preached Goſpel is reſiſted and abuſed, it is " the favour of death," as it contributes to the badneſs of their *ſtate*; as it ſeals and aggravates their de-ſerved *condemnation*. Man's firſt act of diſ-obedience brought death into the world, and all our woe; and on this account, as well as for our actual and acquired depra-vity, a ſentence of condemnation hath gone forth againſt us all. " Curſed is every one that continueth not in all things, written in the book of the Law to do them." From this ſtate of guilt and condemnation, how ſhall ſinners obtain deliverance ? or to what ſhall they look for final releaſe ?—Not to virtues of which they may ſuppoſe them-ſelves poſſeſſed; even theſe, if they had them, are but requiſitions of preſent duty, and cannot make the ſmalleſt reparation for one paſt tranſgreſſion.—Not to vows of fu-ture amendment; for theſe, at beſt, are not only deſtitute of every degree of *merit*, but too often prove precarious, feeble, and tranſitory.

tranfitory.—Not to the juftice of God; for, inftead of peace, that fpeaks nothing but vengeance to the guilty.—Not even to the general, uncovenanted mercy of God; for the utmoft that it can dictate, is, " Who can tell, if the Lord will turn away from his fierce anger, that we perifh not?" Nowhere can fouls, burdened with guilt, find deliverance and reft, but in the method of falvation revealed in the Gofpel. It is only " the law of the fpirit of life in Chrift Jefus, that can free them from the law of fin and death." But if, by unbelief and impenitence, they reject this great falvation, then " the commandment, which was ordained to life, will be found to be *unto death*."

Minifters now, indeed, have no fuch power delegated unto them, as had the priefts under the law, who could declare the incurable leper utterly *unclean :* nor can they pronounce on any of their people, as the Apoftles did on Simon the forcerer, " thou art in the gall of bitternefs, and in the bond of iniquity." No ;—fuch an extraordinary power hath long fince ceafed, with the

caufe

caufe that required it. But it by no means
follows, from this conceffion, that the facred office is now altogether ftripped of its
authority and efficacy. Often perhaps,
though unknown to us, do our fermons, ftill
prove " the favour of death," to fome that
hear us. What Jefus faid of his doctrine,
as dropping from the lips of Prophets and
Apoftles, will apply, in a certain degree, to
that of every faithful Minifter, to the end
of time—" He that rejecteth me, and re-
ceiveth not my words, hath one that judgeth
him: the word that I have fpoken, the
fame fhall judge him in the laft day.*"
Nay, Scripture teaches us, that the hotteft
hell, fhall be the portion of thofe who de-
fpife the Gofpel ; or attend upon it, without any defign or defire to profit : " It
fhall be more tolerable for Tyre and Sidon,
at the day of judgment, than for fuch &c."†

2. The Gofpel, when abufed, proves
" the favour of death," inafmuch as finners, by ftifling and counteracting its fa-

* John xii. 48.   † Matth. xi. 22.

cred

cred influence, only take occafion to *corrupt*
themfelves *the more*, by the abufe they
make of it. This thought admits of illuf-
tration, in various views.—Sometimes, it,
indirectly, *confirms their prejudices.* Coming to hear, with an unfavourable prepof-
feffion of mind againft it, they only attend,
that they may meet with fomething, by
which their difaffection to the truth may be
foftered and confirmed. To fuch men, the
doctrine of *Chrift crucified, the ftrictnefs and
extent of the divine law—the mortification of
the flefh, with its affections and lufts,* are
fubjects peculiarly offenfive. This our Lord
affigns as a reafon, why he fpake fo often
in parables; that perfons who came to ca-
vil at his word, might be hardened and con-
founded.*—Sometimes, *their paffions are ex-
cited by it.* So ftrange a repugnance is there
between the paffions of men and the word
of God, that they often quarrel, both with
the word itfelf, and with thofe who dif-
penfe it. The ftream of depravity being
damm'd up, by the holy law of God, takes

* Matth. xiii. 13.

occafion

occafion, from this circumftance, to fwell and flow, with a more raging fury. Inftances innumerable might be produced of this; but I fatisfy myfelf, with one example from the Old Teftament, and another from the New. In 2 Chron. xxxvj. 15, we fee how the ancient Prophets, as well as their predictions, were fometimes treated; and how the fcorning of the wicked proved unto themfelves, an *evident token of perdition.*—" But they mocked the meffengers of God, and defpifed his words, until the wrath of the Lord arofe againft his people, till there was no remedy." In Acts vii. 54, we fee too, how the faithful preaching of the Proto-martyr Stephen, while it convinced, it fo *exafperated* the Jews againft him, that when they heard what he had faid, " they were cut to the heart, and gnafhed on him with their teeth." And though the punifhment which followed their murderous deed, is unnoticed in the narrative, it is probable, that (Paul excepted) few of them efcaped the juft judgment of God. " If he that defpifed Mofes' law died without mercy : of how much forer

punifhment

punifhment, fuppofe ye, fhall he be thought
worthy, who hath trodden under foot the
Son of God, and hath counted the blood of
the covenant an unholy thing, and hath
done defpite unto the fpirit of grace."*

Again, fometimes, by means of the word,
finners *lull themfelves afleep in carnal fecurity.* While Minifters prophecy to them
fmooth things, all is well; but if, by a ferious and faithful addrefs to the confcience,
they difturb their peace, or detect them in
the *fecret* haunts of iniquity, then they are
offended, and, in proud hoftility, rebel
againft the truth. Were Minifters to over-
look that part of the word, which is more
fearching and fevere, " a difcerner of the
thoughts and intents of the heart," their
preaching would have the moft pernicious
influence; foftering a peace which fhould
rather be difturbed.

To addrefs the precious promifes and
confolations of the Gofpel, unto perfons of

* Heb. x. 28, 29.

C   this

this defcription, is like applying fweetmeats to a difordered ftomach, which tend to feed rather than to cure the difeafe,—to injure, rather than to make the appetite found. By fuch a vague indifcriminate application of the word; many, I fear, have been foothed in their fins, and lulled afleep in carnal fecurity, from which they have never awaked, until " their feet ftumbled on the dark mountains," and till they were about to plunge into the gulph of remedilefs ruin!

But from this dark diftreffing view of things, we turn away—to contemplate a brighter fcene.

Secondly, The Gofpel Miniftry, unto others, is "the favour of life unto life." Were our preaching, my Fathers and Brethren, *univerfally* followed with effects like thofe, we would droop in difcouragement, and in defpondent grief, be ready to relinquifh the very attempt. But although fome of our hearers prove only a fource of *forrow and fhame* to us ; bleffed be God! there are others who prove " *our glory and joy.*"
                                             Although

Although " to them that are loft our Gofpel is hid," or has only a deadly deftru&ive
favour,—there are others whom we may
addrefs, in the language of our Lord,—
" The words that we fpeak unto you, they
are *fpirit* and they are *life*."*

Here, it is natural to enquire, *who* or
what is it that caufeth thefe to differ? Is
the effe& to be afcribed to any fuperior
energy in the word—to any greater exer-
tion of talents in the preacher—or to any
tranfcendent merit in the hearers? No—
they may be children of the fame family,
members of the fame church, may fit, perhaps, in the fame pew, and the preacher
may addrefs them with the fame ability,
earneftnefs and affe&ion : and yet, after all
this equality in outward circumftances, the
one clafs may remain *cold*, *callous*, *lifelefs* as
a ftone, while the other is *awakened*, *melted*,
moved, and *animated* with the livelieft fenfations of faith, love, gratitude and joy !
Upon no other principle, can this happy

* John vi. 63.

difference

difference be properly accounted for, than upon that laid down by the Apoftle, when he faid—" By the *grace of God*, I am what I am."*

-Permit me to illuftrate the phrafe " the favour of life unto life," in *two* diftinct ideas, which it feems to include,

1. That the word of God purely preached, is the grand *inflaument* by which the divine life is ufually infufed and advanced in the fouls of believers.

By nature they, like others, are fpiritually dead; having no vital fenfations, appetites, inclinations, or affections towards God or his fervice. Of the reality and mifery of fuch a ftate, the bulk of mankind have no proper perfuafion. They can conceive of death in no other light, than as it is an extinction of the feelings and functions of animal nature: But that men may be " *dead* even while they live," that even when their

* 1 Cor. xv, 10.

animal

animal and intellectual powers are in full
vigour, they may be deftitute of *moral and
fpiritual life*; is a pofition, fanctioned as it
is by Scripture and fact, which many de-
ride, as the wild reverie of fanaticifm and
folly.* To the eye of *faith*, however,
opened by divine revelation, this feeming
paradox appears at once credible and con-
fiftent. Full well can real believers recol-
lect the time, when the pulfe of facred af-

* Some unenlightened heathen, and infidel Jews have
appeared, who may ferve to affront thofe modern pre-
tenders to *reafon and refinement* in religion.

It is reported of *Socrates*, by his hiftorian, that among
the laft difcourfes which he delivered, he fays, when
fpeaking of *Life*, in this moral fenfe. "Do you afk me
what it is to *live?* I tell you that, to live *truly*, is to endeavour to excel in goodnefs; and to live *comfortably*, is
to feel one's felf growing better and better."

It is faid, too, of *Philo-Judæus*, that, when defcrib-
ing man, fuch as he ought to be, he obferves—"No
one ought to be reckoned a partaker of the *rational* nature, that has not in him *hope towards God.*" If fuch
were the fentiments of men confeffedly ftrangers to
Chriftianity; the *reafon* of thofe alluded to above muft
be fhamefully funk *below the ftandard*; and yet, for-
footh, they would affect exclufively to be thought *rational* Chriftians!!

C 3 fections

fections never beat in their breasts ; when the breath of true prayer never ascended from their lips; when, whatever acuteness, sensibility, and vigour they discovered in prosecuting their *secular* interests, their souls were quite careless, senseless, and dead, as to matters of *spiritual* and *eternal* concern. In this dismal state would they for ever have remained, had not " God, who is rich in mercy, with his great love wherewith he loved them, even when they were dead in sins, quickened them together with Christ."* Though other means may be conducive to this end, the pure preaching of the word of Christ is the grand instrument usually employed, in the renovation of the souls of men. When reading or hearing some particular parts of it, formerly, perhaps, neglected or despised ; the Spirit of Grace, who is the sole *efficient* cause of this change, thereby produces such deep convictions and impressions on the mind, as shew, that " the Gospel is the power of God unto salvation, to every one that believeth."

* Eph. ii. 4, 5.

But

But not only are believers, " of God's own will, *begotten* by the word of truth, that they may be a kind of firft fruits of his creatures ;"—they are alfo *fanctified, quickened, comforted*, and *advanced* in holinefs, by the fame inftituted medium. Perhaps, Chrift's healing the difeafes of many by a *word*, during his refidence on earth, might be defigned to pre-fignify the falutary influence, which his Gofpel fhould have upon the fouls of men. Every blinded underftanding he hath thereby illuminated, every ftubborn will thereby fubdued, every carnal heart thereby purified, every boifterous paffion regulated and reftrained by it, gives frefh atteftation to this truth—that the preaching of the Gofpel, " to thofe that are faved, is *the favour of life.*"

Not only does it produce fpiritual *life*, it alfo promotes fpiritual *livelinefs*. Not more refrefhing to the animal fpirits is fome fweet *odour*, feafonably applied; than are the promifes and confolations of the Gofpel unto a Chriftian, when faint, feeble, and unfit for duty. Under the croffes and calamities of

C 4   life,

life, too, he would be often apt to fink, were he not folaced and ftrengthened by thefe reviving cordials. What David fays of the fweet refrefhment he derived from the Scripture, will apply to the language and experience of every other believer.—" Un-lefs thy Law had been my delight, I fhould have perifhed in my affliction. This word of thine is my comfort in affliction, and in all my ftraits I am revived by it *." Nay, to fhow that this language is not peculiar to one Saint, eminent for holinefs, the whole Church is introduced faying——— " Thy words were found of me, and I did eat them ; and they were unto me the joy and rejoicing of my heart †." On thefe accounts, perfons of the higheft attainments in Religion ftill need to attend on preach-ing, and on other ordinances of the Gofpel: nor fhall they be wholly raifed above this neceffity, until they arrive in the heavenly Zion, where " in God's light they fhall fee light clearly."

* Pfalm cxix. 50. 92.   † Jer. xv. 16.

Which

Which leads me to obferve, as an additional idea included in the text,

2. That the divine life *begun* on earth, by means of the Gofpel, fhall, by the fame means, be carried forward to it's *full maturity* in Heaven.

It is not " a favour of life *unto death*," like the prefent tranfitory exiftence of the body, but " a favour of life *unto life*." It feems to be a general law in the divine conftitution, that there be a gradation, or progreffion, in the works of God. None of them, fo far as we know, are fully compleated, or brought to perfection at once. Every day this may be feen in the various tribes of the vegetable and animal worlds, as well as in the advancement of the human fpecies towards perfection. Thus the feed fown in the earth, by a tedious procefs, arrives at maturity; and the untutored helplefs babe, by degrees, attains to the ftrength an wifdom of manhood.—The fame progreffive plan feems to be obfervēd in the *fpiritual* world. The divine life in the

the foul of man, when firſt infuſed, is, like a grain of muſtard-feed, ſmall and inconſiderable ; others around can ſcarcely perceive it, nay it may be ſcarcely perceptible to the happy poſſeſſor. But ſtrengthened by the word of God, as it's proper aliment, and nouriſhed from time to time by ſupernatural influence, that which was once as an acorn in the field, becomes like a tall tree, in which the birds of the air may neſtle and dwell. That gracious promiſe of the Head of the Church aſcertains both the *means* and the *end*.—" I the Lord do keep it, I will water it every moment ; left any hurt it, I will keep it night and day *." Though the word of God ſhall be rendered unneceſſary, in the heavenly ſtate, it is always uſeful to the Chriſtian, during his continuance here. While here, he is but in a ſtate of *minority* ; and therefore upon the ordinances of religion he muſt punctually attend, as being the proper means of his education, and preparation for his eternal inheritance.

* Iſaiah xxvii. 3.

The

The prefent differs as widely from the future condition of the People of God, as *infancy* from *manhood*. In our prefent ftate of ignorance and infirmity, let us diligently improve divine ordinances, as the means of advancing in our fpiritual ftature and ftrength, " until we all come, through the unity of the faith, and through the know-ledge of the Son of God, to the meafure of the ftature of perfect men, in Chrift Jefus*."

The fubject of the text being thus dif-cuffed, it is now time that I *review and apply* it, in a more direct reference to the fer-vice of the day.

1ft, With what an awful impreffion of it's eternal confequences fhould every Mi-nifter undertake and execute his important office !

If nothing fhort of the vaft iffues of *life and death* are involved in it, it muft require no ordinary fhare of wifdom, piety, dili-gence and zeal, to difcharge it aright. Was Paul, a man of confummate prudence, and
of

* Ephef. iv. 13.

of tranfcendant talents, both natural and acquired, fo ftruck with the work, as to exclaim, " Who is fufficient for thefe things ?" What fhall we think of *their* pre-fumptuous confidence, who, in a diforderly manner, and with very flender furniture, intrude themfelves upon it ! No wonder that fuch raw upftarts, and blind zealots, bring the Miniftry into contempt ; and that the fouls of men run a dreadful hazard, by their petulance and folly. But, when a Minifter duly deliberates on the importance and difficulty of his facred function, and confiders it's confequences as reaching for-ward to eternity, this will ftimulate him to diligence in preparation for it, and to fide-lity in the difcharge of it.

2d. What an air of folemnity, and devout folicitude, fhould reft upon *this Congregation*, on fuch an interefting occa-fion. To you who ftatedly affemble here, this is an *eventful* day ; when you are cal-led, as from an eminence, to look backward on the *paft*, and forward to the *future*. Providence calls you particularly to *reflect*

on

on the many fweet feafons for fpiritual improvement, you have enjoyed under the Miniftry of my much-refpected Father, who has for *twenty-fix* years difpenfed the word and the bread of life among you. You are called to *anticipate*, alfo, the pleafing profpect which this day opens to you, in which the authority, experience, and folidity of *age*, are to be combined with the ardour and induftry of *youth*, for your fpiritual advantage. Therefore,

3d. Suffer, my Brethren, the word of Exhortation.

My counfels fhall be few, and chiefly connected with the fubject of difcourfe; as the reciprocal duties, arifing from your reciprocal relations, will be more fully and forcibly inculcated in the *Charge*. I would only fay,

" Take heed *what* you hear." Be not indifferent to the religious fentiments advanced by your Teachers, as if this were a matter of trivial moment. Truth and error

ror are oppofite in their nature, origin, influence, and effects. Remember the hearing of the Gofpel is not that eafy, indifferent, unintereſting thing, which fome feem
to imagine : it is not like fome fimple me-
dicine, which, if it does no good, will do
no harm ; it is rather like fome ftrong, fo-
vereign remedy, which is only applied
when the cafe is defperate, and which, if
it does *not cure*, will infallibly *deſtroy*.

  " Take heed *how* you hear." Beware
of inattention and drowfinefs—of infenfibility and prejudice—of an over-critical and
cenforious fpirit, in hearing the Gofpel ;
thefe will obftruct your fpiritual improvement, and, of courfe, greatly endanger
your fouls. Guard againft a carnal covet-
ous fpirit ; for a heart petrified by the love
of this world, is a foil into which the good
feed of the word cannot be fown with advantage. Enter the Houfe of God with a
mind open to inftruction, and to the full
influence of the truths you hear, cordially
difpofed " to obey that form of doctrine
that is delivered unto you."

                              " Endeavour

" Endeavour to keep the unity of the Spirit, in the bond of peace." Of the neceffity and advantage of this, I truft you are fufficiently convinced ; if you are not, the hundred and thirty-third Pfalm will give you a lively picture. The prejudices of education and habit, the influence of great names, felf-love, and a fondnefs for fingularity, have in many focieties been an endlefs fource of fchifm and ftrife ; but by your *proved* fidelity ye have fhown, that " ye have not fo learned Chrift." United in fentiment, affection, and practice, I hope, like the primitive Churches, you will continue to walk together in the fear of the Lord, and in the comforts of the Holy Ghoft, and be multiplied. On all who walk according to this rule, " peace be on them, and on the Ifrael of God !"

Continue to refpect, cherifh, and fupport your *venerable* and *aged* Minifter, who has long been the meffenger of the Lord of Hofts to you. Amidft the infirmities of age, and even amid the pangs of diffolving nature, you owe him every tribute of regard ;

gard ; and by rendering it unto him, you
may fmooth the wrinkled brow of affliction,
and help to clofe his eyes in peace.—And,
I demand in behalf of my *young* Brother,
whom I have been honoured to introduce
to you,—the embraces of pure, kind, dur-
able affection—the fympathy, attachment,
and fupport due to one, " who is fet over
you in the Lord,"—and the perfevering im-.
portunity of believing prayer, for a *bleffing*
to accompany all his labours. Yet a little
while, and both Minifters and People muft
" give an account of their ftewardfhip, and
be no longer ftewards"—the *one*, how they
have fulfilled their Miniftry—the *other*,
what ufe and improvement they have made
of all the *grace* that was offered in it. O
that in the joys and triumphs of that day,
both your Minifters may have a diftinguifh-
ed fhare! faying of you, as Paul did of
his charge at *Theffalonica*—" For, what is
our hope, or joy, or crown of rejoicing ?
Are not even ye in the prefence of the
Lord Jefus Chrift, at his coming ?"

I conclude

I conclude by reciting his prayer for *them*, which fhall be my earneft and conftant wifh for *you:* " AND THE LORD " MAKE YOU TO INCREASE AND ABOUND " IN LOVE ONE TOWARD ANOTHER, AND " TOWARD ALL MEN ; EVEN AS WE DO " TOWARD YOU : TO THE END HE MAY " ESTABLISH YOUR HEARTS, UNBLAME- " ABLE IN HOLINESS, BEFORE GOD EVEN " THE FATHER, AT THE COMING OF OUR " LORD JESUS CHRIST WITH ALL HIS " SAINTS.*"—AMEN !

* 1 Theff. iii. 12, 13.

D   THE

THE CHARGE

MR. NICOL.

AT every period, and in every ſtate of things the end of all things, preſents itſelf to view, ſaying, Lo, I am at hand. A child born is in a progreſs toward death ; a building finiſhed has already begun to decay, an union formed looks directly forward to the day of it's diſſolution. In conferring and undertaking a paſtoral charge, the parties are impreſſed with the thought that it muſt ſhortly be reſigned, and an account render- ed. The Chriſtian Miniſter, like Moſes, beholds his charge melting away day by day, and himſelf, though among the laſt, yet moſt certainly, with the reſt, appointed unto death. The ſolemnity of this day ex- hibits the unremitting care of the ever-liv- ing Head and King of the Chriſtian World, to preſerve an uninterrupted overſight of his body the Church ; it exhibits the dig- nified union of a Moſes and a Joſhua ; the one, without repining, ready to communi-

cate

cate a fhare of his refpectability and ufefulnefs to his younger friend; the other, without afpiring, difpofed to divide and thereby
to diminifh the labour, to relieve the anxie-
ties, to mitigate the troubles, and to pro-
mote the views of his aged affociate, in the
moft honourable of all employments. Propitious be the connection to all concerned!

In difcharging my part of the duty im-
pofed, by the appointment of the Prefbytery, on this occafion, I might have fatis-
fied myfelf, Sir, with recommending to
your ftudy and imitation the pattern imme-
diately before your eyes, that of your refpected predeceffor, and now affectionate
colleague. Were he not prefent, I would
have attempted a delineation of that pattern : but I muft not pain his ear with a
reprefentation of the manner in which he
has deported himfelf through the courfe of
a long, acceptable and ufeful miniftry, both
here and in Scotland, though his heart
muft fecretly rejoice in reflecting upon it,
neither muft I expofe myfelf to the fufpi-
cion of employing adulation, even by fpeaking the truth. I refort, therefore, to a ftill
more

more impreffive example, and a ftill higher
authority, by referring you and myfelf, and
all our brethren in the Miniftry, to that
part of the valedictory addrefs of the great
Apoftle of the Gentiles to the Elders of the
Church of Ephefus, which we have re-
corded Acts xx. 26—28.

WHEREFORE I TAKE YOU TO RECORD
THIS DAY, THAT I AM PURE FROM THE
BLOOD OF ALL MEN. FOR I HAVE NOT
SHUNNED TO DECLARE UNTO YOU ALL
THE COUNSEL OF GOD. TAKE HEED
THEREFORE UNTO YOURSELVES, AND TO
ALL THE FLOCK OVER THE WHICH THE
HOLY GHOST HATH MADE YOU OVERSEERS,
TO FEED THE CHURCH OF GOD, WHICH HE
HATH PURCHASED WITH HIS OWN BLOOD.

What adminiftered confolation to the
Apoftle, in finally faying farewel to a Church
which he dearly loved, which he had plant-
ed and watered, furnifhes many a ufeful hint
to you, how to conduct yourfelf in a Miniftry on which you are juft entering.

Could he confidently appeal, at the clofe,
to the office-bearers and members them-

D 3   felves

felves of the Church of Ephefus, refpecting the tendernefs, the diligence, and the
fidelity which he had difcovered in difcharging the truft committed to him? Endeavour, my dear Sir, at every particular
period, and in every particular exercife, of
your Miniftry, to act fo as to lay a founda-
tion for a fimilar appeal ; that at the laft,
when the whole paffes under review, you
may be able to commend and approve yourfelf to the hearts and confciences of all. It
is matter of joy and rejoicing to have the
teilimony of your own mind, that you
have dealt faithfully with the fouls of men,
but it is a very high additional fatisfaction
to enjoy the concurring teftimony of thofe
among whom you have laboured in the
word of the Gofpel ; and what is of ftill
higher impoitance, " of God alfo, how
holily, and juftly, and unblameably, you
behaved yourfelf among them that believe,"
and alfo among them who do not believe.

But what is the fubject of this folemn
appeal ? " I am pure from the blood of all
men." The preferving of the life of a fel-
low-citizen was deemed, in the purer
times of the Roman Republic, the higheft
and

and moft honourable act of patriotifm which
a man could perform. It was rewarded by
a peculiar crown, which entitled the wearer
to a feat among the higheft order in the
Commonwealth, in places of public refort.
To take away the life of another unjuftly,
has, on the other hand, among all civilized,
and even among barbarous Nations, been
adjudged, and avenged as, the moft atro-
cious of crimes. What then is the joy,
what the crown of our Apoftle, in con-
templating, not perifhable life refcued from
the fword of the enemy, but immortal fouls
plucked as " brands out of the burning ;"
not a crown compofed of a few fading
leaves, but an unfading crown of glory ;
not a feat among the Patricians and the
Gods of this World, who are vanity and a
lie, and whofe honours lie rotting in the
duft, but among thofe " that turn many to
righteoufnefs, who fhall fhine as the ftars
for ever and ever ?" And what then is the
atrocity of being acceffory to the murder of
a fpiritual being, formed after the image of
the bleffed God, and capable of never-end-
ing felicity? How humiliating, how alarm-

ing

ing to reflect, in how many various ways
this worft of crimes may be perpetrated!
As the animal life of the man may be de-
deftroyed by ftarving, by poifon, by the
fword, and by other means innumerable, fo
the celeftial fpark, the fpirit that is in man
may be reduced to a ftate of fpiritual and
everlafting death, by with-holding the proper and neceffary aliment, the fincere milk
of the word, and the ftrong meat of the
mature: by infufing the mortal poifon of
falfe doctrine, religious or moral; by the
pernicious influence of feductive example.
Happy the Minifter who can, on a retrofpect, fpeak peace to his foul on this fubject.

By what means did Paul preferve himfelf " pure from the blood of all men?"
He " fhunned not to declare all the counfel of God." What a dignified reprefentation have we here of that Gofpel which we
are commiffioned and commanded to preach
to every creature! " The counfel of God."
It is not a device of the human underftanding; the matured refult of human delibe-
ration,

ration, with all the imperfection of human
ignorance and infufficiency lying heavy
upon it : it is not the partial and tempo-
rary expedient which a fenfe of wretched-
nefs might have fuggefted, but the eternal
" purpofe of Him who worketh all things
after the counfel of his own will ;" a plan
of unerring, efficient wifdom, completely
adapted to it's object, and fulfilling it's defign. This inftructs us, my beloved brother, from what ftores we are to draw the
fupplies which we are, from time to time,
to adminifter to them who hear us.—" The
lively oracles of God," they declare " the
counfel of God." Avail yourfelf, by all
means, of your learning ; avail yourfelf of
the wifdom of paft ages ; avail yourfelf of
your own knowledge and experience ; avail
yourfelf of the counfel of wife men your
contemporaries; but God himfelf alone fupplies the means of melting the ftony heart,
of awakening the flumbering confcience, of
making the broken fpirit whole, of " quick-
ening the dead in trefpaffes and fins." Let
not your fpirit prefume to direct the fpirit
of the Lord, to fupply what you may deem
                              defective,

defective, to rectify what the pride of the schools may confider as erroneous, to explain what is defignedly left in obfcurity. Subftitute nothing of your own in the room of what God hath written, mingle nothing of your own to mar the fimplicity of the truth as it is in Jefus. Nothing is adapted to the neceffities of the foul of man, but the word of life. That ftarving foul cries aloud for bread: Will you give him a ftone? or are you weak enough to imagine that the ftones of a philofophy, " falfely fo called," are to be miraculoufly transformed into the bread of life? He afks a fifh: Will you for a fifh give him a ferpent, to deftroy not to feed ? If God is pleafed to give any teftimony to the labours of his miniftring fervants, it is juft in fo far as they declare " the word of his grace." " The treafure is," indeed, " in earthen veffels," but is for this very end, that " the excellency of the power may be of God, and not of us."

But farther, the Apoftle felt himfelf conftrained to declare not only what *was* the counfel of God, but *all* the counfel of God.

He

He who is employed as a meffenger, and
who acts under a commiffion, muft not exercife a difcretionary power of adding, fup-
preffing, or altering ; if he does fo, he is
chargeable with a twofold infidelity. He
is unfaithful to his employer, whofe exact
meaning he ought to have exactly conveyed
in exactly his own words; and he is unfaithful to him to whom he was fent, who
has an undoubted title to know the exact
purport of what is addreffed to him. Even
Balaam who " loved the wages of un-
righteoufnefs," and was under a violent
inclination to corrupt his meffage, unequi-
vocally declares his affent to this ; " I cannot go beyond the word of the Lord my
God, to do lefs or more :" and again, " I
cannot go beyond the commandment of the
Lord, to do either good or-bad of mine
own mind, but what the Lord faith that
will I fpeak." And the great Meffenger of
Meffengers exprefsly declares of himfelf :
" I can of mine own felf do nothing :—
becaufe I feek not mine own will, but the
will of the Father which hath fent me :"
and, " the doctrine is not mine, but the
Father's

Father's which fent me." In the fpirit of
his divine Mafter, our Apoftle, in like manner, confoles himfelf in the reflection of
having found grace to be faithful at once
to God and to the fouls of men, by keeping
nothing back, nothing that was profitable
·to men, difguifing no truth, palliating no
truth ; and herein he becomes our enfample
to deliver the mind of the Lord, and that
only, " whether men will hear, or whether they will forbear ;" under the tremen-
dous fanction of another apoftolic declara-
tion, refpecting the completenefs of the
word of prophecy. Rev. xxii. 18, 19.
FOR I TESTIFY UNTO EVERY MAN THAT
HEARETH THE WORDS OF THE PROPHECY
OF THIS BOOK ; IF ANY MAN SHALL ADD
UNTO THESE THINGS, GOD SHALL ADD
UNTO HIM THE PLAGUES THAT ARE
WRITTEN IN THIS BOOK: AND IF ANY
MAN SHALL TAKE AWAY FROM THE
WORDS OF THE BOOK OF THIS PROPHE-
CY, GOD SHALL TAKE AWAY HIS PART
OUT OF THE BOOK OF LIFE, AND OUT OF
THE HOLY CITY, AND FROM THE THINGS
WHICH ARE WRITTEN IN THIS BOOK.

The

The expreffion which St. Paul ufes in explaining his own conduct, merits your moft ferious confideration. " I have not *fhunned*," fays he, " to declare all the counfel of God." It plainly implies that he had been under ftrong temptation to foften and to fupprefs. His integrity and candor had expofed him to much oppofition, obloquy and perfecution. Had he dared to diffemble, he might have efcaped a great deal of the enmity which he had to encounter for telling the truth ; but he had counted the coft, and deliberately formed his determination; and at the very moment of his making this addrefs, though uncertain as to particulars of fuffering, he had the near and certain profpect of enduring whatever the malice of bigotry could devife or inflict. AND NOW BEHOLD, I GO BOUND IN THE SPIRIT UNTO JERUSALEM, NOT KNOWING THE THINGS THAT SHALL. BEFAL ME THERE : SAVE THAT THE HOLY GHOST WITNESSETH IN EVERY CITY, SAYING, THAT BONDS AND AFFLICTIONS ABIDE ME. BUT NONE OF THESE THINGS MOVE ME, NEITHER COUNT I MY

LIFE

LIFE DEAR UNTO MYSELF, SO THAT I
MIGHT FINISH MY COURSE WITH JOY,
AND THE MINISTRY WHICH I HAVE RE-
CEIVED OF THE LORD JESUS, TO TES-
TIFY THE GOSPEL OF THE GRACE OF
GOD, Acts xx. 22—24. And it was not
the infirmity of nature, or the defire of ex-
citing compaffion, but an immediate reve-
lation from Heaven of approaching events,
which induced him to add, ver. 25. AND
NOW BEHOLD, I KNOW THAT YE ALL,
AMONG WHOM I HAVE GONE PREACHING
THE KINGDOM OF GOD, SHALL SEE MY
FACE NO MORE.

Through the goodnefs of God, my Brother, you have not to apprehend a ran-
corous, perfecuting oppofition, in fulfilling
the Miniftry which you have received of
the Lord ; on the contrary, you have the
almoft certain profpect of recompence, of
reputation, of fupport, of encouragement ;
you enter on your minifterial career under
every aufpicious afpect of Providence, with
almoft every poffible advantage ; a fair and
unblemifhed character from the fcene of

your

your paft exertions in the caufe of the gofpel ; many feals of an acceptable and ufeful
miniftry; the good will of all your brethren
in the fouth and in the north ; the unani-
mous call of a harmonious and affectionate
people; " other men have laboured, and
you are entering into their labours;" but
ah Sir ! with all thefe in your favour, it is
far from being impoffible you fhould be
tempted to *fhun* to declare all the counfel
of God. There is in gentle natures a reluctance to give pain: the partiality of
friendfhip may blind the eye of the underftanding ; a man who would bid defiance
to the fword of the perfecutor, may be in-
timidated by the fneer of the fcorner; a ftate
of cafe may fuperinduce a ftate of fecurity,
and a ftate of fecurity is ever a ftate of danger : even a man's good qualities fometimes
prove a fnare to him ; hence the importance, the neceffity, of blending prayer
with vigilance ; of adding to the wifdom
of the ferpent and the harmleffnefs of the
dove, the boldnefs of the lion.

Further,

Further, your paftoral care muft be extended to " ALL THE FLOCK OVER THE WHICH THE HOLY GHOST HATH MADE YOU OVERSEER, TO FEED THE CHURCH OF GOD, WHICH HE HATH PURCHASED WITH HIS OWN BLOOD." It is not furely without reafon that the Apoftle deals fo much in univerfals on this interefting oc-cafion. " I am pure from the blood of *all* men :" " I have not fhunned to declare *all* the counfel of God :" take heed to *all* the flock." The good, the chief fhepherd makes no diftinction between fheep and fheep, except fuch as peculiar delicacy of character and condition renders neceffary. " He fhall feed his flock like a fhepherd : he fhall gather the lambs with his arm, and carry them in his bofom, and fhall gently lead thofe that are with young :" and ill does it befit the under fhepherd to fet ftore by diftinctions which his great principal defpifes. In the houfe of prayer, at the table of the Lord, " the rich and the poor," the noble and the ignoble, the learned and the illiterate, the profperous and the difappointed " meet together, the

Lord

Lord is the maker of them all," and they together conftitute " the church of God, which he hath purchafed with his own blood." What, therefore, God hath blended, that let not man dare to difcriminate. Our order is accufed by the world, of fawning upon, and flattering the rich and the great; if this reproach be founded in truth, do what in you lies to wipe it away: if particular refpect and attention are due to any clafs or defcription above another, the wretched of every denomination have undoubtedly a fuperior claim upon him who profeffes himfelf the difciple of a mafter whofe prophetic and hiftoric character it is " to bind up the broken-hearted, to comfort thofe who mourn," and who delivered it as the great teft of his divine miffion, that " to the *poor* the gofpel was preached."

The hands of the prefbytery have this day fet you apart to the holy miniftry, and particularly to the fuperintendance of this flock; but unlefs the Holy Ghoft confirm the defignation, what we have done is a poor unmeaning ceremony, ufelefs to you,

E   and

and unprofitable to the church of Chrift.
But if, as we humbly truft, you " have an
unction from the HOLY ONE," conftituting
you an overfeer of the flock, O then " go
forth another Gideon in this thy might,"
and thou fhalt fave many of the Ifrael of
God out of the hand of the enemy of fouls;
hath not " the Lord fent thee ? The Lord
is with thee thou mighty man of valour."

Once more, eftimate the weight and importance of the Charge you have under-
taken, by the price paid for its purchafe:
" Feed the church of God, which he hath
purchafed with *his own blood*." What pe-
culiarity, propriety, and boldnefs of expreffion! Paul had fuggefted the ftrange idea
of the blood of a foul, meaning its vital
principle, that to the immortal fpirit, which
the crimfon circulating fluid is to the body;
and in order to mark its unfpeakable value,
and to juftify the deep concern which he
took in it, he reprefents the church in general, and the foul of every individual believer, in particular, as redeemed *by the blood
of God*, and capable of being redeemed at no
lefs

lefs a price. What could warrant fuch language, but the truth of the Gofpel hiftory,
and the real character of the Saviour of
mankind? A fpirit, the Father of fpirits,
hath not flefh and bones and blood as we
have, but he who was, and is, God, affumed
flefh and bones, and fhed his blood to re-
deem the foul of man from everlafting
death. O how "great is the myftery of
godlinefs!" "Thefe things the angels defire to look into." "Who can find out
the Almighty unto perfection!" Surely
what God prized fo highly, and purchafed
fo dearly, well deferves your deepeft concern, your moft fervent prayers, your unremitting labours. Does duty at any time
feem painful, and labour fevere? You have
but to reflect thus for a moment, the felf
fame object coft the bleffed Jefus agoniz-
ing pangs, a bloody fweat, the painful and
accurfed death of the crofs; and then every
murmur will be fuppreffed, every bitter
thing will become fweet, and every difficulty difappear, and you will rejoice in
fpending, and in being fpent, in that caufe

E 2   for

for which your great Mafter fuffered, and
bled, and died.

All that I feel now incumbent on me, is
to congratulate my ancient Father and
friend on the comfortable profpect which
opens upon his declining years ; on having
one like-minded with himfelf in managing
the concerns of their common miniftry, on
having the felicity of fharing with him, in
life, the affectionate attachment of a happily united people, and, fhould the courfe
of nature prevail, of tranfmitting to him,
with a departing benediction, the fole charge,
and undivided affections, of an improving,
increafing, edifying church of Chrift. And
I truft his valuable life will be prolonged by
means of the tranquillity which the union
we have been ratifying will diffufe over his
mind, and the dignified eafe and reft which
it will procure for his body. The more it
fhall pleafe God to extend it, the better
I am fure it will be, in all refpects, for his
Timothy, and for their common care, and
for the world.

I feel

I feel myfelf called upon likewife to congratulate this Chriftian fociety on their paft
enjoyments, on their prefent cordiality of
affection toward their minifters and among
themfelves, and on their future profpects.
Thefe are to be the more devoutly acknowledged, and the more thankfully to be re-
joiced in, that a cloud feemed to be ga-
thering, which threatened winter before
the feafon, pregnant with difperfion, alie-
nation and change. But a gracious Providence has difperfed it, and your day fhines
with a redoubled luftre : inftead of antici-
pated winter, you are called to enjoy the
bleffings of fpring and autumn combined.
You have now indeed a twofold object of
regard, but though the perfons are two,
the office, the hearts, the interefts, the exertions, the aim and end of both are one
and undivided ; and one let them be, one
in your refpect, your benevolence, your
efteem, your munificence. Neither, I am
confident, will feel gratified by any mark of
preference conferred upon himfelf at the
expenfe, and to the diminution of the other.
You are happily delivered, as far as human

fagacity

fagacity can give fecurity, from the danger
and inconveniency to which the fuppiy of
a vacant charge is expofed. For intrigue
and cabal, and the various workings of the
felfifh paffions, no room is left. See that
you turn this moft propitious circumftance
to good account. You have only to maintain your exifting harmony, to ftrengthen
the hands and encourage the hearts of thefe
good men, by your prayers, by your fympathy, by your regular attendance upon
their miniftry, and by keeping conftantly
in view the great object and end of the
gofpel miniftry, the falvation of your immortal fouls. This tribute of my gratitude
and affection, will, I hope, be received as
it is meant, for this Church has for many
years been, and ever will be, dear to me;
and I fhall always confider myfelf bound to
wifh, and to pray for, its temporal and everlafting peace and profperity.

And now, my dear young Brother, it
remains that I commend you, and your labours of love, your body and fpirit, your
temporal and immortal concerns to the
great

great Lord of the vineyard, befeeching him
to become to you a fpirit of wifdom to direct, of judgment to difcern, of fortitude to
fuftain, of holinefs to fanctify, and of grace
to help you in every time of your need.
" Now the God of peace that brought again
" from the dead our Lord Jefus, that great
" fhepherd of the fheep, through the blood
" of the everlafting covenant, make you
" perfect in every good work to do his will,
" working in you that which is well-pleaf-
" ing in his fight, through Jefus Chrift,
" to whom be glory for ever and ever.
" Amen."

THE END.

www.ingramcontent.com/pod-product-compliance
Lightning Source LLC
Chambersburg PA
CBHW020242090426
42735CB00010B/1805